MORECAMBE

by Tim Whitnall

‖SAMUEL FRENCH‖

samuelfrench.co.uk

FOR AMATEUR PRODUCTION ENQUIRIES

UNITED KINGDOM AND WORLD EXCLUDING NORTH AMERICA
plays@SamuelFrench-London.co.uk
020 7255 4302/01

UNITED STATES AND CANADA
info@SamuelFrench.com
1-866-598-8449

Each title is subject to availability from Samuel French,
depending upon country of performance.

PERFORMED SONGS

Having received permission from the relevant publishing
companies, the author gratefully includes the lyrics to the
following compositions:

"Positive Thinking"– Tony Hatch/Jackie Trent.
© Copyright 1974 (p28)

"Bring Me Sunshine" – words by Sylvia Dee/music by Arthur Kent.
© Copyright 1966 Music Sales Corporation/Campbell Connelly &
Co. (p41) All Rights Reserved. International Copyright Secured.
Used by permission of Chester Music Limited trading as
Campbell Connelly & Co.

"The Curtain Falls"– Sol Weinstein.
© Copyright Warner Chappell Ltd. ©1962 WB Music Corp
(ASCAP). All rights reserved by Warner /Chappell North America
Ltd (p49/ 50)

Previous productions of MORECAMBE have relied upon the
services of a musical director/associate to realise each song's
arrangement – whether as an orchestrated backing track or
performed live with minimal instrumentation.

Morecambe premiered on August 6th 2009
as part of the Edinburgh Festival Fringe at the Assembly Rooms
Rainy Hall, co-produced by Theatre Tours
International and Anna Murphy for Feather Productions Ltd.

On December 9th 2009 *Morecambe* transferred to London's
Duchess Theatre, co-produced by Michael Edwards and Carole
Winter for MJE Productions, before completing
two national tours in 2010 and 2011.

ORIGINAL CAST/ CREW
Bob Golding – Eric Morecambe (and assorted cast).
Guy Masterson – Director.
James Compton – Musical Director.
Julia Bunce – Costumes/Design/Prop making.

This production earned a 2009 "Scotsman" Fringe First Award
for "innovation and outstanding new writing", going on to
win the 2010 Laurence Olivier Award for Best Entertainment,
Bob Golding himself receiving a personal nomination for Best
Actor in a Musical or Entertainment.

A UK touring production of *Morecambe* began at
the Richmond Theatre on March 30th 2014, co-produced
by Evolution Productions and Feather Productions Ltd,
and directed by Paul Hendy.

INTRODUCTION
by Gary Morecambe

When first I heard about the proposed "Morecambe" play, I was sitting on a beach in Thailand – as you do – with very limited internet service.

I'd received an email from Anna Murphy of Feather Productions, explaining how Tim Whitnall had written a play, which was a journey through my father's life, and that the actor Bob Golding was planning to present it as a one-man show for the Edinburgh Festival of 2009.

My initial reaction, enhanced by the obscurity of my location at this time, was one of horror. How dare someone write a play about my father without coming to consult me at the outset? I can be very protective of all things Morecambe and Wise, and even more so when on the other side of the world and, to all intents and purposes, out of commission.

Fast-forward a couple of months, and I'm sitting in a theatre watching the play for the very first time, and I'm thinking, "thank God they didn't ask me to be involved with writing this play". Reason being: it's a script of genius by a writer of genius. No wonder Tim Whitnall won an Olivier Award for his efforts!

I met Bob Golding, Anna and Tim prior to this, of course, and Bob and I fell in love at first sight. Unfortunately we were both married at the time, so had to settle on becoming great friends.

Bob's courage in taking on the daunting task of playing arguably the most famous comedian Britain has produced was only surpassed by his talent.

In a more recent return to the stage of *Morecambe*, my parents-in-law caught up with it in Brighton, and were gob-smacked by how well Bob captured the spirit of Eric. This is not an impersonation – which, to be honest, is not possible to sustain for around ninety minutes – but a deep analysis of what made Eric Morecambe tick. Added to this is his close examination of all Eric's little gestures, mannerisms and asides, and with the occasional ad-lib thrown in, too. Countless were the times Bob received a standing ovation – certainly every time myself or my sister, Gail, (a stalwart supporter of the 2009 production from beginning to end) were in the audience. A virtuoso tour de force, I think is the standard credit for this type of performance, and one not misplaced on this occasion.

What was fascinating is how emotional theatregoers could be on exiting after the performance. Many were the times they would come up to me in tears to say how much Eric meant to them, and that was always followed by how amazing Bob was in playing him so convincingly.

It could be argued that the play isn't for the faint-hearted; that it was hard to sit through without shedding a tear, or even a bucket-load of them. But the script keeps returning to the humour of the man, counter-balancing the struggle with decades of poor health, and ultimately a far too premature death.

It's such a delight to see Tim's wonderful script in book form, and so right it should be just so. There is nothing I would add, change or suggest to improve this masterpiece, and it is indeed a huge tribute to the one with the glasses, and the sunshine wot he brought us!

FINDING ERIC
by Bob Golding

John Eric Bartholomew... Son, husband, father – oh, and arguably one of the most revered and loved comedians the United Kingdom has ever known. Record-breaking audience viewing figures and an instantly recognisable face, voice and gait. Now study and replicate please.

I must admit if it wasn't for the fact *Morecambe* was such a beautifully constructed script I think I would have been intimidated beyond imagination.

Thankfully I didn't really stop to think about it for too long.

In the creation and journey of the play I have often been asked the archetypal question, "what's it like playing the comedy icon Eric Morecambe." I've never been able to answer the question adequately.

When an actor takes on any role, we get so obsessed with the technical side of playing the part as early as possible in the rehearsal and preparation process. Learning lines and creating the mood of a section and scene in the play, not to mention studying the way the character speaks and moves. So, stopping to take on the enormity and brilliance of the character seems churlish. I spent a long time in this part of the process. It was only when we officially opened the play in Edinburgh 2009, that I (quite literally and audibly) gasped at what I was taking on!

"Just to let you know, Ronnie Corbett and Barry Cryer are in the audience today, Bob!"

In short I think I just tried to simply capture a tiny part of the spirit of "Our Eric". That's all. I'm not even sure if all that character studying and accent analysing made any difference to the end product, because with a beautiful script penned by Tim, and the support of Eric's family and all that laughter on DVD's and anecdotes from friends I was gifted the performance before I even knew I could do it.

It's a privilege and an honour to have played Eric, and what a superb way of doffing one's cap to a personal hero, but let's face it: there'll never be another person who could match what Eric did – and quite right, too.

ONE OF THE FAMILY
by Tim Whitnall

Amongst the many books that Gary Morecambe has written about his father, it was one of the earliest, *Funny Man – Eric Morecambe* that gifted me with an early clue in establishing a theme for my play. Within its pages appears a facsimile of a hand-written letter from Eric's mother, Sadie, sent to him on his twenty-first birthday, not only affirming her love for him but also effectively setting her only son free, wishing that "the sun may always shine" for him. I am forever grateful to Eric's family for granting me permission to include Sadie's letter, not only because it appears at a tipping point in our story (see p.17), but also because it underlines the significance of *family* for Eric along the entire crazy-paved footpath of his life. As *Morecambe* illustrates, he would grow up determined to take care of his own wife and children, tirelessly punching the clock and putting in a shift the only way he knew how...

Those fabulous, far-off Saturday evenings, when not just *with* our families but <u>as</u> families we would howl at the "Stripper" sketch or Eric and Ernie's heretical take on Grieg's Piano Concerto, belong to a time when television could be relished as a collective experience. Perhaps it's that which makes those memories all the more precious to those of us who lived through them.

As a nation we regarded Morecambe and Wise as our own: from us. For us. About us. The headline in *The Times* announcing Eric's death in May 1984 emphasised that proprietorship, describing him as "ONE OF THE FAMILY TO MILLIONS". Only Eric Morecambe could have left an "Eric Morecambe-shaped hole" in our lives.

PRODUCTION NOTES

MORECAMBE is a one-man performance, every role being played by the same actor. As the play evolves he dips in and out of key moments, inhabits his own very personal memories, and quite often engages in passionate conversations "with himself". The actor must be able to sing, dance, bond with a ventriloquist's doll, play musical instruments, credibly re-create each character and possess excellent comic delivery and timing.

Additional dialogue is provided by pre-recorded sound cues, notated in this draft along with relevant sound effects and/or. The author acknowledges these titles are subject to copyright controls and has included them in this draft for information purposes only.

SETTING/TIMING

Time and place are suspended, creating a mood of magic and mystery.

The piece runs for approximately 90 minutes, excluding an interval.

CHARACTERS

The lighting state creates a rarified, ethereal atmosphere – time transfixed.

Up stage centre a false proscenium evokes a vintage music hall with plush tabs, a small stage and footlights.

At down stage right a theatrical props trunk. At down stage left two old-fashioned theatre seats, a side table, a coat stand and tailor's mannequin – a female torso.

Houselights go down and a sound effects cue – BBC radio pips – segues into a news bulletin from 28th May 1984.

NEWSREADER *(voiceover)* The comedian, Eric Morecambe, has died at the age of fifty-eight. Mr Morecambe who, with his partner Ernie Wise, formed one of Britain's most successful ever comic duos, had been appearing last night in Tewkesbury and is thought to have suffered a heart attack immediately following his performance. Attempts to revive him proved unsuccessful. The Prime Minister said that the country had lost "a genuine national treasure" and that Morecambe and Wise "had brought joy and laughter to millions throughout a long and illustrious career"...

The up stage tabs ruffle as **ERIC MORECAMBE**, *about to make one last stop on his celestial odyssey, huffs and puffs behind them unseen. He calls:*

ERIC Mum? Mum?

His head pokes through the tabs about six feet higher than it should do. (N.B. He is actually standing on a concealed stepladder behind them.)

Mum? Are they in? *(Aside)* They're all drunk, the lot of 'em. I can smell it from here! Pardon? What d'you mean, "Hit 'em with the good stuff"? I haven't got any!

He enters, resplendent in specs, mac and flat cap; daft walks and "ya-ta-ta-tas" abounding, chomping on an unlit pipe and lugging a battered suitcase. Almost subliminally he massages his left arm, clearly causing him bother. Gazing around at his unfamiliar surroundings, he calls for his wife:

Joan? Joanie?

No reply. Returning to the tabs he opens them and yells:

Ern?

Slightly disquieted, he defaults to "clown mode", pretending to be throttled by an arm protruding between the tabs – ERIC's own, of course.

I've always said if it weren't for Venetian blinds it'd be curtains for all of us. Curtains for all of us! Ahem.

Puts down suitcase, crosses stage left and peruses the theatre seats. Across them lies a female mannequin's leg with a pink bow tied around it. Picks it up and studies it.

Well, I never! A Christmas gift for Angela Rippon... It's not her main present – just a stocking filler.

Audience groans.

Have another drink.

Tosses leg into the wings. Spots a bottle of Johnnie Walker whisky on the side table.

Think I might join you. Johnnie Walker. I know him well. Makes you feel double and act single. I'm partial to a small scotch – you've met Ronnie Corbett...

Next to the bottle, he espies a human skull.

Blimey! Peter Cushing's lost some weight!

Picks up the skull, coming over "all Shakespearian".

Alas poor Peter. Me and Ern still owe him ten guineas.

Growing more confident in his odd, unearthly surroundings – the purgatorial stage of his heavenward journey – ERIC *strides into the spotlight.*

Your honour's players, hearing your amendment... *(Aside)* Can we say "amendment"? Pardon? I'll smash yer face in!

(To audience) Are come to play a pleasant comedy. For so your doctors hold it very meet; seeing too much sadness hath congeal'd your blood, and melancholy is the nurse of frenzy. *(Coughs)* Arsenal! Therefore they thought it good you hear a play – wot I did not wrote – and frame your mind to mirth and merriment which bars a thousand harms and lengthens life. William Shakespeare – *The Taming Of The Shrew.* Or was it *Paint Your Wagon?* What do you think of it so far?

AUDIENCE RUBBISH!

ERIC *(to* SKULL*)* What did they say?

Manipulates the SKULL*'s jaw, "venting" badly:*

SKULL Ruggish!

Humming and shuffling, ERIC *crosses to his prop trunk, opens it, drops the skull into it then screams before pulling out a Des O'Connor album. Hyperventilating, he replaces it, rummages, and produces a working ventriloquist's doll – a* perfect *likeness of* ERIC*'s lifelong comedy partner* ERNIE WISE.

Well Ern, here we are, pally. Right back where all the trouble started. A big, dark room with lights in it. The roar of the greasepaint, the smell of the crowd. Not like the cold world outside; Lancashire chill, in off the Irish Sea, deep as the black seam, turn you bluer than a miner's skin. Oh, yes. In here it's different. In here, you stand a chance. Soft, plum velvet, gold leaf dripping everywhere like melted butter.

Places ERNIE *on one of the seats, moving to hang his coat and cap on the stand – but missing it completely. Underneath, he reveals a knitted tank top, shirt and tie, making him look more boyish. He also deftly swaps his spectacles for a pair of 1930s "regulation roundies".*

Bated breath of Hindel Wakes and warm stout, hotpot and stale tobacco. Expectant, expec*ting*, check your fly…and on you go…

Mounts the stage, reminiscing:

The footlights grill your shins; spots fry your eyeballs as you squint up to the Gods, Hell-bent on a blessing.

Sound effects: applause/cheers.

Listen Mum, they're clapping! Louder than Gatlin guns, wounded on the punchline, rocking backward for a gulp of air!

THREE PUNTERS *react:*

PUNTER 1 Look at 'is gormless face!

PUNTER 2 Have you seen the lad do Robb Wilton? Swear blind it were 'im!

PUNTER 3 Wait 'while you hear the one about whippet and t'vicar!

ERIC And then Mum's voice hissing from the wings. That pink, pudgy prawn-of-a-finger reeling in her only child.

SADIE Jifflearse! Get off! Leave 'em wanting more, else they'll round on you like a stung bulldog. I'll see to it you're never tied to a whistle like your dad, Eric. Now you see to it you give everyone a business card.

ERIC *(to audience)* "Master Eric Bartholomew, Vocal Comedy And Dancing Act, 43, Christie Avenue, Morecambe". Spit-sopped hanky wiping off the greasepaint, a poke of chips and the bus back after. Half a crown a week she scrapes together to pay for my lessons: music, dancing and singing. Pity really 'cos I can't play a note, can just about dance and can never sing in tune! She calls me "Jifflearse" on account of the fact that I can never stay still. She's even bought me my own plank, genuine oak so's I can brush up on my tappin'. Your proper jumping Jack. And the gift of the gab?

Tries out a joke on his father, **GEORGE.**

'Ere, Dad, have you heard? Cop shop toilet's been pinched?

GEORGE Oh aye?

ERIC The police have nowt to go on!

GEORGE Fair funny is that, son. Have a barley twist.

ERIC *(to audience)* If he hadn't have been so shy I'd have probably been born two years earlier! Swung a pick and spade for Morecambe Corporation he did, happy as a sandboy 'till the day he retired.

GEORGE T'int right you follow me, son. You should listen to your mother. She knows what's what. There's a seed in you, Eric. Your beanstalk up to a better life.

ERIC *(to audience)* Ten years old, Fridays at the Billiard Club, tables for stages, "Blue Moon" on green baize at five bob a throw... *(Sings)*

BLUE MOON, YOU SAW ME STANDING ALONE...

HALL OWNER Oy! Tap shoes off on't tables, Four-Eyes!

ERIC Sorry mister. *(To audience)* And as for school...

HEADMASTER Master Bartholomew, out of forty-nine pupils, you have attained the lofted position of forty-fifth. D'you not nurture any inkling of ambition, boy?

ERIC I want to play football sir, but I've got two problems – both feet! *(To audience)* The only lesson I enjoy is learning how to smoke. I couldn't tell you who crossed the Red Sea but I know why the chicken crossed the road. My education can't be found in books...

Leaps back onto his stage.

"Kiss Me Goodnight Sergeant Major" on the pier and "Lily Of Laguna" for courtin' couples under it. Old folks home for pie and peas... My granddad knew the exact day, place and time he would die. He weren't psychic, the judge told him! Elms Hotel, ten bob... I wouldn't say me room is damp, but this mornin' I found a goldfish in the mousetrap!

HOTELIER Oh, he's a cracker, your Eric. We'll have him back a week Wednesday.

SADIE I'm afraid Eric's booked solid for three weeks. But you can have him after for twelve bob a night.

ERIC Twelve bob a night!? Takes Dad a week to earn thirty! Barracks dinners, garden fetes, lidos and legions, and then...

Sound effects: a **LIVERPUDLIAN M.C.** *(pre-recorded) announces:*

M.C The Kingsway Cinema, Hoylake proudly presents the "Melody Maker" Search For Talent, 1939. Our first finalist hails from the Naples Of The North: Morecambe, Lancashire. He's here – but he's not all there – Eric Bartholomew!

Finding a beret and a tatty old set of tails in the trunk, **ERIC** *pulls them on and climbs onto the stage, redeeming a (preset) ukulele from behind the tabs.*

ERIC *(sings)*
I'M NOT ALL THERE, THERE'S SOMETHING MISSING
I'M NOT ALL THERE, SO FOLKS DECLARE
THEY CALL ME LOOBY, LOOBY
NOTHING BUT A GREAT BIG BOOBY
POINT AND SAY, "THAT'S WHERE YOU WANT IT"
BUT THEY KNOW THAT'S WHERE I'VE GOT IT
I KNOW THEY THINK I'M SLOW
LET THEM THINK, LET THEM THINK, I DON'T CARE
SOMETIMES I RUN ERRANDS FOR THE FOLK UP AT THE GRANGE
WITH A FIVE POUND NOTE THEY TRUST ME
P'RAPS YOU'D THINK THAT'S STRANGE
BUT THEY NEVER CALL A POLICEMAN
WHEN I SAY "I'VE LOST THE CHANGE"
'COS I'M NOT SUPPOSED TO BE ALL THERE... CUCKOO! CUCKOO!

Sound effects: applause.

(To audience) I did it! I only went and blinkin' well won! What's the star prize, Mum? Summat I can eat or swap? Summat I can set on fire, is it? Oh. An audition in Manchester for bandleader and impresario Jack Hylton. *(Flatly)* Brilliant.

SADIE Now you listen to me, lad. This world owes you nowt. Like I've always told you: "Put in the elbow grease, else you'll be a ha'penny more than a lad from Lancashire". D'you think George Formby was born with his little ukulele in his hand? You're going to Manchester and that's that. Pull it off and I'll buy you an airgun.

ERIC *(reprises enthusiastically)* 'Cos I'm not supposed to be all there!

Pumped up by his mother's promise of a new firearm, he swaps his ukulele for a Chaplin-esque walking cane from behind the tabs – the perfect prop with which to ramp up his efforts.

Right, Mr Hylton. Why don't I give you the lot, see if I can't knock your hat off? *(Deep breath)* "Zing Went The Strings Of My Heart". Words nice and clear, shuffle-ball-change. I want that airgun. Bang! "Never Let Your Braces Dangle". Unclip mine so they do, hike up strides at last second. Smile, don't forget the balcony, their money's as good as the four-and-sixpennies. Does it come with pellets, I wonder? Bang! "Top Hat, White Tie and Tails". Where's me blinkin' cane? Soon be pickin' off beer bottles from the back wall. Bang! Last one now, my piece de resistance... "Lily Of Laguna", down on one knee, arms wide as Morecambe Bay. Give him both barrels, sunshine. Bang, bang! *(Pause)* He's clapping, but not a lot, and who's that sat next to him pouring syrup into his ear? Blow me, it's his West End Wonder Boy, the "Mickey Rooney of Leeds" – Ernest Wiseman!

Crosses indignantly to **ERNIE** *on his theatre seat.*

What d'you mean, you were "only nudging him to keep him awake"? *(To audience)* Hitler has invaded Poland by the time my call-up papers arrive.

Produces a telegram from his pocket, reading:

"Youth Takes A Bow", Nottingham Empire. Stop. Jack Hylton! Pleased if Eric should join show. Stop. Touring salary, five pounds per week. Stop. *(To audience)* And I am an airgun richer... POP! Twice nightly, six nights a week. Dickie "Large Lumps" Hassett...

LARGE LUMPS I've got enough money to see me through to the end of me life – if I die at six o'clock tonight!

ERIC "Two-Ton" Tessie O'Shea making her entrance on an elephant...and dear old Arthur Tolcher and his mouth organ...

Yanks a harmonica from his pocket and plays a few bars of **MUSIC: "SPANISH GYPSY DANCE".**

(aside) Not now, Arthur, not now. *(To audience)* Girl singers, boy singers, acrobats and tumblers...and me. Bournemouth Winter Gardens, Bradford Alhambra, Bristol Hippodrome, loving every minute of it. Nothing is going to rain on my parade, not even the Führer.

Sound effects: a bomb descends, whistling.

SADIE 'Ere, Eric. Have you heard? There's a new boy joining the cast in Swansea.

ERIC A new boy? Who's that then Mum?

SADIE Ernie Wise.

Sound effects: bomb explodes.

ERIC The little doodle-bugger! Ernest Wiseman... The blighter's changed his name! That junior sensation from "Band Waggon", song-and-dance man by seven, stage and radio star at thirteen, joining us?

MUSIC: "I'M KNEE DEEP IN DAISIES" – INSTRUMENTAL.

A green-eyed **ERIC** *observes* **ERNIE** *from the wings.*

Look at him, cock-sure as a bantam, trilling away like a flamin' skylark. "I'm Knee Deep In Daisies"? Should be *elbows* deep in "shorthouse's" case.

ERNIE Hah-hah. Not tonight *sonny*, for I'm standing on a toadstool.

ERIC "Sonny"? *"Sonny"?!* Oh no, look at him dance! Gliding over the boards with all the power and grace of a bloody Spitfire. He's got it all. I hope it's terminal. And hark at that lot lapping it up like kittens.

WELSH PUNTER We're lucky to 'ave 'im, boyo, given the ravages of current hostilities, isn't it?

ERIC *crosses to coat stand, hanging up his beret and tails.*

ERIC *(to* **ERNIE***)* Bighead! And you wear long trousers, and you are on seven pounds. Seven pounds? The powdered egg I could buy with two quid extra! I call you "Lilywhite" 'cos I can't find anything wrong with you. The daft thing was, I find out you feel the same about me. What a pair of dunces. Oxford is about to educate us...

Sound effects: a knock.

I'm not answering, Mum. It might be the Jerries!

SADIE Good. I can strangle 'em with this scarf I'm knitting.

ERIC That's how it starts – the knock in the night.

SADIE I'll knock you in the night, you soft clot.

Opens the door to discover a forlorn **ERNIE**.

Ernie, love! You look frozen solid! Come in. You've nowhere to stay? I'm not surprised with all these bloomin' soldiers everywhere bedded down for the night. You're welcome here, love. I'll sleep in the single bed and you can climb in the double with our Eric.

ERIC *(horrified)* Me? Sharing a bed with 'im?

SADIE Well, it'll save us all a pretty penny.

ERIC *(to audience)* Ern's mum has drilled into him that his bankbook is his best friend, so he jumps in with me quicker than a turpentined cat.

Sits beside **ERNIE**, *pulling a blanket over them both.*

But, once under the covers, we find out that we make each other laugh. A lot. We both love Abbott and Costello, Laurel and Hardy, Hope and Crosby. In no time we are messing about in dressing rooms, swapping gags on trains and doing silly voices into the small hours. We can't stop laughing...

SADIE Honestly! I wish you two would put all this mucking about to good use. I don't see why you can't let off some of this steam in front of an audience. You know enough daft jokes between you. Find a song or two. Form a double act.

Eureka. **ERIC** *picks up* **ERNIE** *and leaps onto the stage.*

ERIC Click! Lightbulb over bonces. Tricky in a blackout. *(To* **ERNIE***)* I'll be Bud, you can be Lou. "Can I have a pound of sausages? Lean? *(He leans)* Can I have a pound of sausages?" Live and breathe the act, work our behinds off and keep mum 'till we come up with something.

MUSIC: "BY THE LIGHT OF THE SILVERY MOON" – INSTRUMENTAL.

"Careless talk costs live acts", and all that. Did you hear about the dog in the flea circus? He stole the show! Keep going, we're onto something now... Four weeks to work up four minutes... We're ready, Ern! Thanks for letting us audition, Mr Hylton, Bartholomew and Wise ready to change your world. Gags and patter in the American style, the old soft-shoe and the "Silvery Moon". Wahey! Be honest...

Heads down stage right and sits **ERNIE** *on the trunk.*

JACK HYLTON Be honest? I will be honest. Your jokes went out with Disraeli, your stage name doesn't exactly trip off the tongue and I can't abide "By The Light Of The Silvery Piggin' Moon". *(Beat)* Liverpool Empire. You're on this Friday.

MUSIC: *vaudeville-type sting.*

ERIC *grabs* **ERNIE***, taking him back onto the stage.*

ERIC My girl told me I should be more affectionate. So I got two girlfriends!

Sound effects: laughter.

ERNIE What smells of vinegar and giggles? A tickled onion!

Sound effects: laughter grows.

ERIC Did you hear about the thief who stole the calendar? He got twelve months!

Sound effects: belly laughs/enthusiastic applause.

Ern, I can see their teeth! Listen to them, they like us, they really like us! Look at my mum, she's crying. And Mr Hylton was clapping too – his head's a-bob! Well, boss, did we do OK?

JACK HYLTON Highly impressive, lads, highly impressive. How d'you fancy going on again next week?

ERIC D'you hear that Ern? Thanks Mr Hylton. Where are we?

JACK HYLTON The Glasgow Empire.

*Sound effects: thunder and lightning/ **MUSIC: "CARMINA BURANA".***

ERIC *(to audience)* Max Miller used to say, "Play the Glasgow Empire? I'm a comedian, not a missionary". With our feet on the plank, the theatre fireman prods us with his cutlass...

THEATRE FIREMAN Rest assured lads, if they like you, they let you live. It's a miracle if we can get 'em to toast the Empire at the finale, so nae jokes about football, Rabbie Burns or the Pope. There's nae need to look so feared. "Still waters ne'er made a skilled sailor".

ERIC Still waters? Oh God, Ern, I'm seasick already.

MUSIC: "SCOTLAND THE BRAVE".

That's overture and beginners... Two accordion players and a monkey in a kilt! How the 'eck are we going to follow that?

*Sound effects: a **SCOTTISH M.C.** (pre-recorded), booming and portentous.*

SCOTTISH M.C. And now from South Of The Border, two young comics up here for the very first time. England's newest hopes, Bartholomew and Wise!

ERIC *gulps as the spotlight hits him.*

ERIC I never knew a monkey could do *that!* My wife is the most wonderful woman in the world. And it's not just my opinion – *she* thinks so too!

Sound effects: a lonesome wind.

Talking of girls, Ernie once went out with a girl who had a terrible stutter. By the time she said she w-w-wouldn't, she already h-h-had!

Sound effects: a solemn church bell peals.

As for my girl, I know I can count on her – she always wears beads. It's the abacus Madam, you see…counting…beads… Ern, is that my heart or is Buddy Rich on the bill with us?

Shuffles towards wings.

Keep smiling, Ern…and for God's sake – keep walking. Only ten more yards… Feels more like ten miles! Couldn't we hail a cab to the wings?

They reach safety.

Oh, Mr Fireman, are they always that quiet?

THEATRE FIREMAN By the sound of things, they're beginnin' tae like you.

Relieved, **ERIC** *places* **ERNIE** *back on his theatre seat.*

ERIC *(to audience)* Out of Glasgow – alive; Scunthorpe, a new gag here; Aston, a song there; Grimsby, one more *tiny* beat before the punchline…

JACK HYLTON Eric, Eric, Eric…

ERIC Mr Hylton, Mr. Hylton, Mr. Hylton?

JACK What the hell are we going to call you, eh?

ERIC Call me?

JACK Bartholomew is terrible.

ERIC It's been terrible all my life, Mr Hylton.

JACK HYLTON How about Bartlett? Once knew a pawnbroker called Bartlett. Bartlett and Wise? No. Barton as in Dick

Barton, a touch of daring? No. Berwick? Eric Berwick? It's even bloody worse! It's a problem, right enough...

ERIC *(to audience)* Problem solved in Nottingham – and it's not often you can say that. Cue big, burly American vaudevillian performer – Bert Hicks...

BERT HICKS *steps forward, all swagger and poise.*

BERT Mrs B, I got an actor friend, name of Eddie Anderson, found himself in an identical situation to your boy. Eddie's from Rochester, Minnesota. Now calls himself "Eddie Rochester". So, where are *y'all* from?

ERIC *Morecambe* and Wise!

Inspired, he crosses to the trunk, pulling out a blazer and boater and donning them with panache.

(To audience) Blue blazers and straw boaters, gaberdine strides with a crease you could slice crumpets on, hand stitched loafers, spotlights a-glint on toetips. Let us sing for you, "Only A Bird In A Gilded Cage" perhaps? Marvel at Ernie's unmatchable Jimmy Cagney... "You dirty rat...you dirty rat...". We'll trip the lightest of the most fantastic for you, and as for our jokes...

Confidently steps up on to the stage.

My wife was sent to me from heaven – as a punishment!

Wrong move. Incensed old-stager **SCOTT SAUNDERS** *confronts* **ERIC.**

SCOTT SAUNDERS You thieving little bastards, half-inching an old pro's one-liners!

ERIC Sorry Mr. Saunders. *(Aside)* Scott Saunders, veteran of variety! We were only borrowing it from you, sir. An homage.

SCOTT SAUNDERS An 'omage? Is that right? Fair enough, you can have it for a week, but tell it after that and I'll be ripping off more than your material!

ERIC *(to audience)* Next time we try it – a stony silence. The old gimmer had gone out there and told the joke himself just before we'd come on.

SCOTT SAUNDERS Ha, ha! Lesson one, kiddiewinkies: never kid a kidder.

ERIC *(to audience)* Lesson two: nothing is original until you make it your own. *(To* ERNIE*)* We've got work to do, Ern. Push, push, push 'till we get it right. Do it again until we can do it in our sleep and... I was rubbish in school... Do it again and... All I could do was smoke... Do it again until we know where the laughs come... What's going to happen to us when we're not kids any more?... And – STOP! What the hell d'you think you're doing, Ernie? We agreed on the timing of that punchline and you haven't learnt it. You're not a bit of good!

ERIC*'s mother intervenes.*

SADIE John Eric Bartholomew! I haven't brought you up to speak to people like that, least of all Ernie. Leave this room and don't come back until you've calmed down.

ERIC *sits beside* ERNIE.

ERNIE Mrs B, Eric is only trying to make me the best feed in the country, and I'll tell you something else – he's going to be the best comic in the British Isles.

ERIC *(to audience)* After that, we never have another cross word and we shake on two things: everything we earn gets split right down the middle, and it must never matter which of us gets the laughs. Right from the very beginning. *(Beat)* 1942, the act up to seven minutes – ten if we talk slowly. Ern and I are up and running; at least we think we are, but the war has taken its toll, and youth its final bow.

Sound effects: telephone rings.

ERIC *mimes answering after first ring. It rings a second time.*

Ern! How are you? Working on a coal round? Things looking black, eh? Me? Razor-blade factory. Business not too sharp. I'm going crackers, pally. Never thought I'd pine for "I'm

Not All There". Pardon? What do you mean, "there's a way back"? A new show hiring at the Prince of Wales? They'll book us on the spot!

Sound effects: a steam train puffs down to London.

Mimicking it, ERIC *"puffs" from stage right to stage left.*

(To audience) And I wasn't wrong. The producer does book us on the spot: as a couple of walk-ons, totally uncredited. But, we're getting ten quid a week and *Strike A New Note* becomes a hit. Hollywood big-shots come to watch every night: Jimmy Stewart, Clark Gable, Alfred Hitch-er, Hitch…

ERNIE Hitchcock?

ERIC He may have, I didn't notice.

Waggles his spectacles playfully.

(To audience) And there are even girls! Girls without their mothers knitting in the wings – that's a revelation to me! Steady on, Bartholomew. Remember what your mum says: "marry a girl, and your fourpenny pie'll cost you eightpence". But, wouldn't you know it, just as London is beginning to look like our steak and kidney…

MUSIC: "REVEILLE".

ERIC *removes blazer and bow tie, hanging them on the coat stand. Takes a miner's helmet from it and puts it on.*

National Service. Ernie into the Merchant Navy shipping coal, me down the mines supplying it – ever the double act. Nobody tells me that Accrington Pit had been condemned to closure…

Crawls along a dark, foreboding tunnel.

Sound effects: hammers and picks.

This filthy tunnel can't be more than two foot high. Please God, don't let it cave in on me. Up at 5.30, back after dark. Just a lad from Lancashire now, doing his bit for King and Country. Keep digging, tearing the skin from your hands and bruising everything from arse to elbow. Keep digging, Bevan Boy, chew on that coal dust and suck in the black air. Dig, dig, dig...

Pulls himself upright, addressing a military doctor.

Oh doc, doc, you've got to help me... I can't breathe properly. Got these funny thudding pains in my chest and I've started...sweating...cobs. What d'you reckon? Nothing too serious, eh? Just a touch of heart trouble, you say? You're going to classify me "C-3"? Unfit for service? *(Beat)* Wa-hey! *(Happily)* Mum, Mum...they say I'm unfit for service.

Drops his miner's helmet behind the seats.

SADIE The only coal botherin' you Eric, should be the stuff drivin' that train back down to London. Come on, there's work to be done...

Sound effects: a steam train puffs <u>back</u> to London.

ERIC *"puffs" from stage left to stage right.*

ERIC *(to audience)* Finding a hole for half a double act isn't easy, trawling the papers and rapping on agent's doors 'till our knuckles have turned to pickled walnuts. One long, cold day, Mum and I are traipsing down Regent Street when...

ERNIE Oy, Jifflearse!

Delighted, ERIC *crosses to* ERNIE.

ERIC Lilywhite! Now that's a hell of a coincidence! Mum and I have found digs in Chiswick. You? Sharing a flat in Brixton with a Chinese acrobat? Who said variety was dead?

SADIE Ernie, love, there's a bed with your name on it at our place. You two might as well be out of work together as separately...

ERIC *(to audience)* My mum sees something of herself in Ernie: determination, business savvy and he really does care about me. On my twenty-first birthday, she writes me a letter:

MUSIC: a wistful **"BRING ME SUNSHINE"** *– INSTRUMENTAL UNDERSCORES.*

ERIC *produces* **SADIE***'s letter from his pocket and reads aloud:*

"I know at times you have thought me hard but I have had to do it for your own benefit. Now you are your own boss and I sincerely hope you have learned a little from my nagging. I don't want to be sentimental but I just want you to know how we both love you and tried to do our best, and though to the world you are a man, to us, you will always be our baby, so don't get any big ideas! From now on I do not interfere with whatever you do, but if you want advice, well of course we will be there. Remember the world is yours for a football and may you score many goals. So I close now, once again saying "thank you, Eric" for giving us so many happy memories and causing us no worries. May the sun always shine for you, love."

Pockets the letter, picks up **ERNIE** *and crosses down stage centre.*

(To **ERNIE***)* Right. Just me and you against the world now, pally. Pay our dues, put in the shifts and slave over any hot audience who'll have us. *(To audience)* A travelling circus – six in one night and they're cub scouts! Pubs, saloons, masonic halls and seamen's missions. In fourteen months, we work for a grand total of...six weeks. Our landlady, Mrs. Duer, tells us: "Just pay me when you can". Without such kindness Morecambe and Wise would flap home to Morecambe and Leeds like two soggy homing pigeons. *(To* **ERNIE***)* This new "television thing" will take over, you'll see. Dick Emery, Michael Bentine, Peter Sellers – straight out of the armed forces and into nightclubs stuffed with agents and big-nobs from the B.B. Bloomin' C. Ern, I want to feel some of that wind in our sails...

MUSIC: seedy nightclub piano.

The Windmill Theatre, Soho – the "Big Smoke". *(To* **ERNIE***)* Look at these dancers! Legs up to the Lake District and feathers over Fleetwood and Filey. Those girls bat so much as an eyelash and they'll shut this place down in a flash. 'Ere, what's that bloke up to in the front row? Trilby down, collar up and newspaper cross his lap? That's one hell of a twitch – or a very angry ferret under his *Daily Mirror!*

Sound effects: a gruff, grubby **COMPERE** *(pre-recorded)*
announces:

COMPERE Thank you, gentlemen. We trust you enjoyed our
presentation, "Fräuleins Of The Frankenwald". Laughter
now...

Sound effects: groans.

...and those two peppy northerners, Moreton and Wise.

Having changed into a smart jacket and bow tie (preset)
behind the tabs **ERIC** *appears on the small stage up stage right,*
holding **ERNIE**.

ERIC Felicitations, music lovers! Hey mister, can I borrow your
paper when you've finished with it? Actually, don't bother,
I've gone right off "Spot The Ball". I wouldn't say that
dancer had long legs but that was real snow on her head!
Ernie needed a stepladder to light her Balkan Sobranie!

Zero reaction.

Blimey, hasn't anyone told them the war's over? *(To audience)*
Thud, gag after gag. Flat on its backside. Thud, a seat
vacated. Bombs of failure. A fat man snores. Someone
clears his throat – I hope it's his throat! The manager of
the Windmill Theatre, Vivian Van Damm – or "VD" to his
friends – has no qualms...

VIVIAN VAN DAMM *reacts:*

VAN DAMM I've seen people having more fun in a morgue than
putting up with you two. You can finish the week, then I'll
have to replace you I'm afraid.

ERIC And he does replace us with that other fellow. What's his
name? Tony, er, Tony...

ERNIE Hancock?

ERIC He might have, I didn't ask.

Waggles his specs again.

Well, Ernie, it's been nice working with you...

Places him atop the trunk.

(To audience) Wednesday – Throat Clearer, Thursday – Trilby Man, Friday – Snorer and Trilby Man, Saturday, our very last show – Throat Clearer, Snorer, Trilby Man and...

Pulls a briefcase from the trunk. A dapper, fast-talking gentleman enthusiastically introduces himself.

GORDON NORVAL Gordon Norval, booking manager. I enjoyed your performance immensely, rich in pith and vigour. Tell me chaps, what do you know about "Fig Leaves And Apple Sauce"?

ERIC Sounds like one heck of a Sunday lunch.

GORDON NORVAL Another nude revue, over at the Clapham Grand. You couldn't fit me in this Monday, could you?

ERIC We'd fit you in *last* Monday if we could, Mr Normal!

GORDON NORVAL Oh splendid. Oh super. Oh marvellous. I'll have the contract drawn up. Two spots, ten minutes each?

He exits cheerily, dropping his case back in the trunk.

ERIC *picks up* **ERNIE**, *suddenly gripped by fear.*

ERIC Two spots?! We've barely enough material for one! Oh Ern, we're finished!

ERNIE Fear not, my friend, I know just what to do.

ERIC You do?

ERNIE I do. A little bird told me...

ERIC Bird? What kind of bird?

ERNIE *(cryptically)* Why, a certain woodpecker...

ERIC Oh well, what's another ten minutes? Do I smell nervous, Ern? Don't answer...

Sound effects: music hall atmosphere.

On you go, pally... Break a short, fat, hairy leg...

MUSIC: "THE WOODY WOODPECKER SONG" – INSTRUMENTAL.

Jumping behind the drape up stage right, ERIC *thrusts* ERNIE *between them, leaving him alone on stage.* ERNIE *dances away, cheerful and chirpy as* ERIC *narrates from behind the curtain.*

Good old Ernie. Five feet seven inches of Pennine Stone, nerves of blue steel. I'd worry if I didn't have anything to worry about. Right, Eric, prepare to kiss it all goodbye. Again…

He bursts through the curtains, grinning insanely and, perfectly on cue, guffaws the Woody Woodpecker laugh, shoulders vibrating in tandem.

Sound effects: audience roaring approval as ERIC *sings.*

(sings)
UH-HUH-HUH-HA-HA! UH-HUH-HUH-HA-HA!
IT'S THE WOODY WOODPECKER SHOW,
UH-HUH-HUH-HA-HA! UH HUH-HUH-HA-HA!
IT'S THE WOODY WOODPECKER SHOW!

Sound effects: riotous laughter/applause.

ERIC *whisks* ERNIE *down stage left, sitting him back on his theatre seat.*

Ern! You genius! It only went in as filler…*killer!* What's that, Mr Normal? Two-and-ten a week extra? And the Kilburn Empire wants us too? *(To* ERNIE*)* Pinch me, Ern. *(Gooses)* Get off. Morecambe and Wise – shake hands with The Big Time. "Front Page Personalities", the Moss Empire circuit and the Mets. Forty quid a week and forty gags in ten minutes, and our first, real live agent…

FRANK POPE, *epitome of a Tin Pan Alley "ten percenter", appears.*

FRANK POPE Eric, Ernie – or should I say "esteemed clients". Ever enjoyed playing the Empire, Swansea?

ERIC "Enjoyed" is not the word.

ERNIE Actually, Mr. Pope, that's where Eric and I met.

FRANK POPE Good. You can meet there again Friday, second on the bill. And I've got you a nice little booking on "Variety Bandbox". It's the wireless mind, so see you both put on a tie.

ERIC hoists a vintage radio from the trunk, twisting its "on" knob.

Sound effects: ERIC*'s voice (pre-recorded) emanates from the speaker:*

Thank you, thank you, ladies and gentlemen. And now, in response to a number of requests Ernie and I have received – goodnight!

Sound effects: applause/laughter.

ERIC guffaws, replacing the radio in the trunk. Crosses to ERNIE.

ERIC *(to* ERNIE*)* Ah, there's no sweeter sound, eh Ern? Not even you and your enchanted fountain pen could put into words how it feels to win that applause...

He starts pacing, patently restless.

That churning inside, like your guts are trying to take a bow themselves, that bubble of joy in your throat and a beam broad enough to split your mug in half. Everything we've worked for, eh? All those years, all those miles. All we ever dreamed of...

ERNIE Eric. What's the matter?

ERIC What do you mean?

ERNIE Mrs Duer's going to bill us for that hole you're wearing in the carpet.

ERIC Oh Ern, I wouldn't trade our success for anything, but I can't help feeling that there's something missing. It's like...

ERNIE You're not all there?

ERIC Very funny. Ever thought about becoming a comedian?

ERNIE I'm serious. The higher we climb, the more empty it all feels?

ERIC *(to audience)* How does he do it? He should charge. *(To* **ERNIE***)* You should charge.

ERNIE You need someone with whom you can share all this. Who'll understand the tears behind the laughter.

ERIC And the cigarette behind the safety curtain?

ERNIE The thinker inside the clown.

ERIC And the dirty underpants inside the suitcase?

ERNIE It's as plain as the hair on my head.

   ERIC *lifts* **ERNIE***'s fringe. Is it a wig?*

ERIC There's no answer to that.

ERNIE It's time for you, Eric, to take to the floor in "The Dance Of True Love".

   MUSIC: *a romantic waltz.*

   ERIC *replaces* **ERNIE** *on the theatre seats and heads up stage left where he twirls with the tailor's mannequin.*

ERIC *(to audience)* A Monday morning bandcall at the Edinburgh Empire. Look at her! Head, shoulders and everything else above the rest of the chorus line Joan Bartlett – the voice of an ostrich, the legs of a nightingale...sorry – other way round! Miss Margate, 1951 – and it's difficult to miss Margate *any* year! Our eyes meet across a crowded orchestra and this vision gazes back with only one thought on her mind:

JOAN There stands before me the last man in the world I'd ever consider stepping out with.

ERIC *(to audience)* But tentative ticker ne'er won tasty twirler... *(aside)* and you should have heard that in rehearsal!

   He gingerly approaches **JOAN***.*

Er, Miss Martlett... Bargate... Joan. May I interest you in a cup of coffee? Oh, you're going shopping? Oh yes. Trying to find a gift for your *boyfriend?* Oh no. Why don't I help you? I like buying men presents. I'm one of them myself. A man that is, not a present, but if you play your cards right, you could always unwrap me later – wa-hey! *(To audience)* Over the weeks, a few more coffees, a floppy sandwich and a cheeky chuckle or two. Miss Bartlett is starting to nicely defrost in the blast furnace of Bartholomew's masculine charms.

Rapidly slaps the back of his neck.

11th December, 1952. Morecambe and *wife...*

MUSIC: "THE WEDDING MARCH".

Hitched Sunday, London Palladium, Monday, Sheffield, Tuesday. *(Aside)* I always thought it was Sheffield Wednesday... I don't write this stuff, you know, I just say it! ... Sheffield on Tuesday to start the honeymoon – sorry – pantomime. Christmas cheer, New Year bountiful, Ernie following my lead and marrying himself. Well, not *himself*, but a dancer named Doreen. 1953 stretches out before us like a road cobbled in ingots.

A different crowd every night, "Workers' Playtime" on radio, Blackpool for summer season. The very best of times, eh Ern? We're young, we're in love and we believe we can live forever!

Sound effects: telephone rings.

ERIC *mimes picking up after the second ring. It rings a third time.*

Oh Joan, my darling wife. I love you so much. I know I'm always telling you. I love you, Mrs Morecambe. I've done it again. How's Margate? It's raining in Blackpool, still, brings 'em in off the Prom... *(Checks his watch)* No, I've got five minutes. We're not on 'till after the plate spinner...

Sound effects: breaking china.

Blimey love, we're on! Listen Joany, there's a really good chance me and Ernie are going to get given our very own series on the tel... Tell? Tell me? Tell me what?

Sound effects: a baby cries.

(To audience) The midwife is sure it will be a boy. Nine months after we get hitched our daughter, Gail, arrives. I mix some cement, spread it over our drive and write in it with a stick, "Thank you Joan, I love you".

Heads to coat stand, swapping his jacket for a grey tux and clip-on bow tie.

If I'm guilty of putting her on a pedestal then I'm happy to be holding the step ladder. She'll be beside me all the way: for richer, for poorer, for better – and for worse...

Sound effects: (pre-recorded) **BBC ANNOUNCER:**

BBC ANNOUNCER   And now the BBC television debut of Morecambe and Wise, two snappy jesters tipped for the very top. Join them now as this quick, slick pairing hit the ground "Running Wild"!

Sound effects: cymbal crash/applause.

Picking up **ERNIE**, **ERIC** *heads jauntily down stage centre to make their big debut before the TV cameras.*

ERNIE   Thank, thank you. So nice to be here, ladies and gentlemen...

ERIC   And when you've been round at your mother-in-law's, it's nice to be anywhere.

ERNIE   Is that where you've come from?

ERIC   Can't you tell from the bruises?

ERNIE   How long did you stay?

ERIC   About five feet, ten inches – before the rack.

ERNIE   Anyone would think you didn't get on.

ERIC   With Mussolini in a farthingale? I've had more fun with measles.

ERNIE Surely, these are just teething troubles?

ERIC Teeth *are* the trouble. She's knocked mine out!

Perches **ERNIE** *on the trunk, pulling out a newspaper, reading:*

"Why on earth millions of viewers had to be given this sort of stuff I just don't know… TV's worst effort for months". "Morecambe & Wise's flop of a show…their gags were weak…". We didn't even write them! "Their sketches corny." They even hire a bloke to tell our audience when to laugh! One review – *The People* – I clip and keep in my wallet for posterity. "Definition of the week: TV set: the box in which they buried Morecambe & Wise". Ern's broken out in boils and my poor mum is refusing to show her face in public.

Crosses to side table and pours himself a scotch.

Depression? Stress? The only word I know for it is "failure". *(To* **ERNIE***)* Oh, pally, our dream is turning into a nightmare…

He sips his whisky, sits and dozes.

MUSIC: *a celeste underscoring; ghostly, disquieting.*

ERIC *dreams of himself as a* **CIRCUS RINGMASTER** *proclaiming:*

CIRCUS RINGMASTER One more for the high-wire! Don't forget your pole, lad, and mind how you go.

ERIC *stands, miming a precarious walk across a high-wire.*

ERIC *(to himself)* A tap dance on a greasy tightrope, any joker could do it. Far below me, boiling and growling, hungry and thundering: "The Fatal Falls of A Man Who Isn't Funny Anymore". Toes on steel, cold, slimy like snail-silver. Grip that bar, Bartholomew…one step…two… I can't do it…only one foot on the wire… I'm falling…

He channels **SADIE***, calling to him through his subconscious.*

SADIE Jifflearse!

ERIC Mum!

SADIE Give us your hand, Eric! Give us your hand and you'll be alright.

ERIC Pull, Mum! Pull us in!

ERIC's dream now transports him to a deserted thoroughfare.

On the other side an old music hall stands, shut and shuttered, chunks of brick breaking off, falling, exploding into clouds of red dust...

SADIE They're all closing now, Eric. Tearin' 'em down to make way for supermarkets and office blocks.

ERIC And on a wall a curling playbill reads: "TV's Greatest Disappearing Act – Morecambe & Wise!" No... No-o-o!

Wakes with a start, rattled, pausing to breathe.

Harry Secombe reckons a disaster can be good for a comic. "Every knock chips an edge off you" *(blows a Secombe-esque raspberry)*. Me and Ern have had that many knocks we've got the edge of a blancmange!

Crosses to **ERNIE**.

We'll be thirty before we know it pally, over the bloody hill.

ERNIE Well, let's wipe the slate clean and start all over.

ERIC What do you mean?

ERNIE Get back to what we know best. The big, dark room with lights in it – roar of the greasepaint, smell of the crowd.

ERIC That's my line!

ERNIE *Our* line. Our stock-in-trade. Morecambe, Wise–

ERIC –and a living, breathing, paying audience. You're right! Let's hibernate like two squirrels and not poke our noses out 'till we've a hoard of new chestnuts – hellfire, a brand new act! I want to tickle the mayor's wife up there in her box...

Scampers up onto the stage.

I bought my wife a fur coat made from hamsters. Went to Blackpool for the day – couldn't get her off the big wheel!

Sound effects: laughter.

(To ERNIE*)* Get that vicar down front wobbling his dog collar... "Remember there are seven deadly sins – that's one a day – have a good week, father! "

Sound effects: more laughter.

(To ERNIE*)* And have the whole dress circle join in on the punchline...

Little Ernie – a comic from Leeds,

Once swallowed a packet of seeds,

In a month, silly ass,

He was covered in grass...

(To audience) Altogether now...

And couldn't sit down for the weeds!'

Sound effects: stomping/wild applause.

ERIC *crosses to the trunk, finds another newspaper and reads it:*

"Could this really have been the same Morecambe and Wise we endured on television? Watching them last night was akin to witnessing the release of a dormant genie after a protracted incarceration inside his lamp. It can only be a matter of time before this talented twosome properly make their mark in t...te...tel..."

ERNIE Television is the future, Eric.

ERIC It put us back ten years.

ERNIE We weren't ready. If we don't aim for the gogglebox now we might as well give up.

ERIC *(strategising)* Right. Right. We'll never again tell a joke we don't find funny. If we can't impose our personalities on a sketch, it isn't going in. Deal?

ERNIE Deal.

ERIC *(to audience)* Ernie is being smart. Morecambe has to get Wise.

MUSIC: "POSITIVE THINKING".

ERIC *picks up* **ERNIE,** *whisking him down stage centre to sing.*

WHEN YOU FEEL DOWN TRY POSITIVE THINKING
THAT'S WHAT I'M TOLD THE MAN SAID
DON'T WEAR A FROWN, TRY POSITIVE THINKING
LAUGH AT YOUR TROUBLES INSTEAD
THIS CRAZY WORLD THAT WE LIVE IN
WILL KEEP ON SPINNING ROUND
BUT WITH GOOD, STRONG POSITIVE THINKING
WE'LL GET TOGETHER AND LIFE WON'T LET US DOWN…
WHEN YOU FEEL DOWN, TRY POSITIVE THINKING
THAT'S WHAT I'M TOLD THE MAN SAID
DON'T WEAR A FROWN, TRY POSITIVE THINKING
LAUGH AT YOUR TROUBLES INSTEAD
YOU'VE GOTTA LOOK ON THE BRIGHT SIDE
ON HOPE SO MUCH DEPENDS
WITH YOUR CONFIDENCE SINKING
POSITIVE THINKING
HELPS YOU ON THE WAY, MY FRIEND…

ERIC *and* **ERNIE** *mount the fake stage up stage centre.*

WHEN THINGS LOOK BLACK, TRY POSITIVE THINKING
TREAT EVERY SEASON AS SPRING
NO GLANCING BACK, TRY POSITIVE THINKING
TRUST WHAT TOMORROW MAY BRING
THIS CRAZY WORLD *WHAT* WE LIVE IN
WILL KEEP ON SPINNING ROUND
GOOD, STRONG POSITIVE THINKING
GOOD, STRONG POSITIVE THINKING
GOOD, STRONG POSITIVE *DRINKING*
WE'LL GET TOGETHER AND LIFE – WON'T – LET – US…

ERNIE *(sings)*
DOW-W-W-W-W-W-W-W-W-W-W-W-W-W-N!

ERIC I wish I could sing like that, don't you?

Blackout

End of Act One

ACT TWO

MUSIC: "FOLLOWING YOU AROUND" – (INSTRUMENTAL).

ERIC *pokes his head through the upstage centre tabs, grinning. As the music continues, a black patent leather shoe pokes through the drapes, followed by a sock, suspender and trousered leg. It grows longer and longer, reaching a ridiculous length before* **ERIC** *reprimands it.*

ERIC Hey! Go on, get off! Get back to the Isle Of Man. The Isle Of Man!

The leg swiftly retracts behind the curtain.

ERIC *re-enters in a smart mohair suit and tie. His spectacles too have been upgraded to 60s "American Classic" rims.*

Sound effects: telephone rings.

ERIC *won't be caught out this time. Smugly anticipating three rings, he counts on his fingers: one... Two... Silence. Warily he mimes picking it up and, sure enough, a third ring ensues.*

Joan? I'm worried sick. I need you more than...

Sound effects: a thud/ woman's scream.

...this knife thrower needs new spectacles. And a new assistant. Joan, there's a good chance that Ernie and I will be offered another crack at appearing on te...tel...tell... Tell me? Tell me what?

Sound effects: a baby cries.

(To audience) The midwife stakes her Premium Bonds on it being another girl. Sure enough, our son, Gary, is born just

29

before I go back in front of the firing squad – sorry – *the cameras* at the Wood Green Empire.

A flamboyant **ATV DIRECTOR** *hoves into view.*

ATV DIRECTOR Eric. Darling. Relax. It's only a television series.

ERIC You're right, Mr Director. Sir.

ATV DIRECTOR Winifred Atwell's the star. Let her take the weight.

ERIC Now there's a thought. *(To himself)* Calm down Bartholomew, stop smoking. And don't have any cigarettes either.

ATV DIRECTOR Just be yourselves and let Cyclops come to Odysseus. Right everyone... Mr Morecambe, Mr Wise... Your places please for the "The Taxi Driver and the Drunk" sketch. Going in 5, and 4, and 3, and 2, and...

Sound effects: a taxi engine idles.

ERIC *(drunk) sits on the sofa beside* **ERNIE** *(taxi driver).*

ERNIE Where to guv'nor?

ERIC My place please, driver.

ERNIE Any clues?

ERIC It's made of bricks with a tiled roof and lots of lovely windows. Hic!

ERNIE Do you know the road?

ERIC I do. It's the very same one my house is in!

ERNIE Which area?

ERIC Fock-costers.

ERNIE "Fock-costers"? Never 'eard of it.

ERIC It's at the end of the Diccapilly Line. Hic! You've no idea where you're going. Let me off right here!

ERNIE How about a tip?

ERIC Certainly my good man – get yourself a road map.

Sound effects: cymbal crash/applause.

ATV DIRECTOR And...we cut there. Super. Thank you, ladies and gentlemen, thank you floor. We have in fact gone to the commercial break.

His earpiece rattles, making him jump.

Wait! Gremlins, you say? A technical hitch? *(To* **ERIC** *and* **ERNIE***)* Darlings, we're still on... Live to the nation... Eric, treasure, for God's sake, save us!

ERIC Pardon?

ATV DIRECTOR Ad-lib...improvise...make something up!

ERIC Such as?

ATV DIRECTOR I don't know, dear... Just be yourself!

ERIC *grins cheesily "to camera".*

ERIC Ahem. That's right folks, we're still here. So are you, by the look of it. You didn't think you'd get shot of me and Ern that easily, did you? This isn't the BBC, you know.

Sound effects: titters.

That's us, folks. Me, Mr Eric Morecambe and my tiny friend Ernest Wise. He's half a star, you know – the only man I know who doesn't have to bend down to tie his shoelaces! I tell you something, it's a miracle Ern got to play our taxi driver... He's a terrible driver. His feet hardly reach the pedals. In fact, he's only just recently passed his driving test – on a donkey.

Sound effects: more laughter.

Taxi!

Sound effects: riotous laughter.

ERIC *picks up* **ERNIE** *and sits him atop the prop trunk.*

Now, I get it, Ern. I really get it. Like the man said, "Be yourself", and treat the one-eyed monster as if it were just another member of our audience...

ATV DIRECTOR Boys, boys...what can I say? So fresh! So funny! So you! We'd love to have you back next week...and the week after...

ERIC ... And the week after that, and we're tickled to add three new words to our billing: Direct. From. Television.

MUSIC: a James Bond-type sting.

(To audience) Jermyn St. Piccadilly, the H.Q. of an elite organisation. A blue fug clears and there he sits; silent, suave behind a mahogany desk bigger than our caravan. The mohair suit, cufflinks the size of manhole covers and a smouldering Dunhill he keeps tapping over his shoulder...

Sitting on the theatre seats, enigmatic theatrical agent BILLY MARSH *meets* ERIC *and* ERNIE *for the first time.*

BILLY MARSH The name's "Marsh", "Billy Marsh" – special agent. Television, gentlemen, can be a comic's worst enemy. Frankie Vaughan sings an old song, the viewers stay tuned, but if a comedian tells a joke they've heard before...big black screen, little white dot. The only way to stop them turning off is to keep turning them on with new material. If you think you can do that, I, gentlemen, can get you all the television you want...

ERIC *(to audience)* A rainbow of colour-coded telephones fans out in front of him, each a hotline to a crock of gold. Green – ATV, blue – BBC, red... *(To* BILLY MARSH*)* Who do you ring on that one, Mr Marsh?

BILLY They ring you.

ERIC *(to audience)* He picks up the green one and secures us a guest spot on *Star Time*. In a trice, *Saturday Spectacular*, and *Sunday Night At The London Palladium*...

MUSIC: brassy walk-on sting.

BRUCE FORSYTH *appears in his classic "thinker" pose.*

BRUCE FORSYTH Thank you ladies and gentlemen, nice to see you, to see you nice! So much nicer than last week's audience... I want you all to put your hands together and give a lovely warm Palladium greeting to the nation's favourite double act... Morecambe and Wise!

ERIC Thanks, Brucey. *(Aside)* You can't see the join. *(To audience)* "The nation's favourite!" And, up in Morecambe, Sadie Bartholomew tucks into a nut cluster and brushes away a tear as she watches me and Ern – at last – busting through the barrier.

Sound effects: telephone rings.

Ern! Look! It's the red one!

BILLY MARSH *pulls out a (preset) red telephone receiver, taking a call from* **SIR LEW GRADE.**

BILLY Ah, good morning, Lew. Morecambe and Wise? The possibility of their very own series? I see...

Pause.

I see.

Pause.

I see.

ERIC *(to* **ERNIE***)* As long as he sees, eh?

BILLY Mr Grade says, ahem, "you're joking – those two? I wouldn't give *them* a series". *(Into telephone)* So, Lew, what news regarding this ghastly industrial dispute? "Any act holding an Equity Card won't be allowed to work for ATV? Really?"

ERIC *(to audience)* He's tappin' that Dunhill again.

BILLY Of course, er, such restrictions wouldn't apply to members of the Variety Artists Federation, would they?

Pause.

I see.

Pause.

I see.

Pause.

ERIC Good eyesight, this fella.

BILLY Of course the boys are up to date with their subs...ahem.

Replaces the telephone.

Mr Grade says he would be delighted to offer you your very own series.

MUSIC: "TWO OF A KIND" – INSTRUMENTAL.

ERIC *collects* **ERNIE** *and heads down stage centre, soft-shoe shuffling in delight as the theme tune to their hit ATV series rings out.*

ERIC *(To audience)* And *we* name it *Two Of A Kind.* That's us alright, eh Ern? Rhubarb and custard...

ERNIE Crosse and Blackwell...

ERIC Brahms and Liszt...

ERNIE Speak for yourself, I never touch it when I'm working.

ERIC You call *this* work? *(To audience)* Soon, the only ratings beating ours are *Coronation Street's*! We're the highest paid double act in Britain, they've given us a BAFTA award – and a second series! The Rank Organisation want us to star in three films! We're going to cut our own album at Abbey Road, and some group called The Beatles are guesting on our show... *(Aside)* He-llo Beatles. *(To audience)* Get voted "Showbiz Personalities Of The Year"... That's *us*, not John, Paul, George and Bongo... *(Over his shoulder)* Alright Bongo?

Sound effects: a drum fill.

(To audience) Wa-hey! 1964, off to CBS Studios, Manhattan, two thousand miles from the Scunthorpe Savoy. We step off the plane, Ernie in his element and me inside a sick bag... Taxi!

Sits, a garrulous **YELLOW TAXI CABBIE** *talking over his shoulder.*

CABBIE Don't tell me, don't tell me – Australia? Oh, Lancashire and Yorkshire – you're *Scottish!* So, you're on the Ed Sullivan Show, huh? What are ya? Actors, opera singers? Lemme guess – you's the organ grinder and the little guy's ya monkey? Ha! I should be the show! So, have you guys met Mr Sullivan? He saw you on the Royal Variety Performance? Well, over here, it's Mr *Television* who's the royalty. The white Rolls Royce, two suites at the Delmonico Hotel... Whatever Sullivan says goes. If Ed don't like what you're doing in rehearsal, you may not make the broadcast...

Sound effects: a timpani roll as ED SULLIVAN *(pre-recorded) announces:*

ED SULLIVAN Now, ladies and gentlemen, those highly amusing European comedians... Morrey, Cambey and Wise!

ERIC *(to audience)* I had no idea there were *three* of us! Fifty-three million viewers and "Mr Television" cocks up our names. We hit 'em with a few tried and tested gags, a song and dance, but it's like whacking your a head against a brick wall. They ask us back *seventeen* times, but I never get the feeling they ever think we're truly funny – ask the *Daily News*... "Morrey, Camby and Wise should remain England's problem, not ours". Bob Hope says that we talk too fast for the viewers. Unless it's them thinking too slowly. I've grown quite attached to being England's problem. It makes you wonder though whether comedy only jumps the pond one way. Let's face it, Ernest; you and I will never be meatloaf and Martinis. We're pie, we're peas and we are "Do Like To Be Beside The Sea"...

Sound effects: seagulls, waves, funfair sounds.

(to audience) From Broadway...to Great Yarmouth. Box office records getting smashed, genuine laughter from a genuine audience and a whole summer with my family right beside me all the way. Life is sweet again. In early 1968, our contract with ATV expires. Lew Grade offers us a generous renewal. I yap like a Jack Russell, roll over, tongue a-lolling... But Ernie says:

ERNIE Not unless our fans can see us in colour.

Sound effects: an atomic explosion.

ERIC *(to audience)* Mushroom cloud of cigar smoke. Fallout.

LEW GRADE You'll have colour when I say you have colour.

ERIC *(to audience)* So Lew's beloved nephew, Michael...

Sound effects: fanfare.

...who just *happens* to be working as an assistant to our agent – what a coincidence – puts in a call to the BBC who would love to sign us up and can guarantee us our very first colour series. It's "adieu, Uncle Lew" and "toodle-pip" to red telephones.

Paces left and right; urgent, purposeful.

Now, everyone wants us everywhere, day and night. Club dates and garden fetes... "Come and meet so-and-so", "can I be on your show?" More records, TV shows, trips abroad, eight weeks in Glasgow...

Pauses, anticipating thunder and Carmina Burana, *but this time they don't materialise.*

...a killing pace, but if we don't keep it up, everything dies. We can work every night if we want to – and we want to. "Bank raids", we call them. Two funny fellas off the BBC with a road-tested, copper-bottomed stage act...

Suddenly, unexpectedly he grabs his left arm, gasping.

The pain shoots through me like a punch from a rivet gun, but it can clear off to the back of my mind. This is Batley. This crowd wants sunshine, dammit. Keep going. Tuesday feels like a clog dance in treacle; Wednesday, pushing water uphill with a tennis racquet; Thursday...but every laugh gives me a boost, ups the ante. *(Flatly)* Keep. Going. You. Fool.

Sound effects: **ERNIE**'s *voice (pre-recorded).*

ERNIE *(voiceover)* Eric, let's call it a night.

But **ERIC** *pushes on.*

ERIC *(to audience)* I hope you enjoyed your scampi. The chef here does a marvellous job for a man with his skin condition!

ERNIE *(voiceover)* Eric, you're not well.

ERIC I wouldn't say he was unhygienic, but the only time chef washes his ears is when he eats a slice of watermelon.

ERNIE *(voiceover)* Eric, take it easy.

ERIC Chef's food will always have a special place in my heart... burn.

The laughter rings in his ears, the lights dazzle him.

(To himself) Heartburn. Drink and a lie down, that'll do it... hotel thirty miles away...

Takes off his jacket and sits, the theatre seats now "becoming" his car.

Hold on to that steering wheel... *(Gasps)* Daggers a-jabbing inside my ribcage...find those digs like I've always done. Quarter to two in the morning...street lights, orange blur... This looks like Leeds... City varieties, Vesta Victoria... Pains in my back now, much worse...rubber band round my chest...pull over, window down...there's a bloke over there... Hello...

Elderly passer-by **WALTER BUTTERWORTH**, *as Yorkshire as an Eccles cake, responds:*

WALTER Th'alreet lad?

ERIC Not really, no. Where's the hospital?

WALTER Th'ospital?

ERIC The place where sick people go.

WALTER Oh, th'infirmary! Tha'll need to go back on tha' sen, take first left up by t'bridge, second right after Bricklayer's, through to traffic lights past abattoir. Then it gets a bit complicated...

ERIC You couldn't drive me there, could you?

WALTER Ooh, I'm in't Territorials. I've only ever driven a tank before.

ERIC Oh well, this, my friend is a Jensen Interceptor. It'll drive itself. *(To audience)* After one wrong hospital, several wrong turnings and two wrong doors, my good Samaritan eventually gets me to "th' infirmary". A nurse yanks down my strides and inserts a two-foot needle into my fundament. Not a pretty sight.

ERIC lies back, exhausted.

The pain eases…cool, sacred air fills my lungs again and I lie there alone…all alone…never been alone… Where's my Joan?

WALTER Eric?

ERIC I'm on the gurney. Is that you, Ernie?

WALTER It's me, Walter Butterworth.

ERIC Who?

WALTER The bloke who drove you here. You look exceedingly pale lad, not well at all. Now, none of me pals will believe 'owt of this, so I were wonderin'…tha' couldn't just sign us an autograph, could thee?

ERIC Pardon?

WALTER You know, before you go…

ERIC chuckles, appreciating the irony.

ERIC *(to audience)* Les Dawson once said, "being a comic is no joke". It's fear that spurs you on; fear of failure; fear of the "heard that one before" or seeing your name slide down a bill until it's smaller than the printer's. And the greater the success, the tighter the grip. There's only so much juice in the orange. You're sure you can handle the squeeze then the next minute you're waking up in an oxygen tent…

Sound effects: ERNIE (pre-recorded) speaks.

ERNIE John Eric Bartholomew. You'll do anything for a laugh!

ERIC Ernie. I'm so glad you've come.

ERNIE I see you got the flowers.

ERIC Such a lovely wreath.

ERNIE And the grapes?

ERIC A little sore, but settling down nicely, thanks.

ERNIE Eric, my dearest chum. About that tenner you owe me...

  ERIC *chortles.*

ERIC *(to audience)* Business as usual. But after Ernie leaves my bedside, Joan tells me that he breaks down and bursts into tears...

Pulls a dressing gown from behind the sofa, stands and dons it.

The little fella ploughs on, popping up on chat shows and radio interviews, launching our jokebook and sporting a badge saying: "Eric's Getting Better! (P.S. I don't feel so good though)". Every single penny he makes, he sends me half. I can't tell you what that means to me. Ernie is keeping Morecambe & Wise on life support.

Sound effects: birdsong gently trills.

Do excuse me, won't you?

Takes off his trousers, revealing socks held up by suspenders.

I can feel myself slowly getting better. I start walking, birdwatching, even playing the odd round of golf. The coffin nails get knocked on the head and under strict medical advice, I take up...a pipe.

Produces a pipe from his robe pocket.

Summer is long and warm, perfect for a spot of fishing.

He mimes casting a rod and line.

It's good, this spare time lark, isn't it?

Sees a familiar face and waves, calling:

Morning Matron. It's nice out, isn't it? I may take mine out later. Pardon? Am I what? Am I taking my pills like a good boy? Oh...

Rummages in his pockets and finds a prescription.

(Reads) "Take four tablets three times a day. Store medication...in fridge".

At down stage right a small fridge miraculously appears from the wings.

Look at that. No expense spent.

Crosses and opens fridge.

MUSIC: "THE STRIPPER".

He takes out a pill jar, tipping four tablets into his hand. In tempo with the music he tosses them one by one into the air, catching them expertly in his mouth. Finally, defiantly, he tears off his dressing gown, and tosses it into the wings, pushing the fridge off with it.

I grow strong and chipper, ready to begin again...

Crossing behind the theatre seats he changes into a (preset) black tux, bow tie, trousers and the classic "ERIC MORECAMBE specs".

MUSIC: "ALSO SPRACHT ZARATHUSTRA".

August, '69. Bournemouth. One small step for man, one giant leap for Morecambe; my first appearance since Batley...

Collects ERNIE – also changed into a tux – from stage right wings and takes him down stage centre.

As Ern and I walk out from the wings, the most amazing thing occurs...

Sound effects: tumultuous applause.

Two thousand people leap to their feet, roaring and clapping. It must last five minutes. It's as if the whole country has turned up to let us know they're missing us, they want us back and for Eric and Ernie, the best is yet to come...

MUSIC: "BRING ME SUNSHINE".

With a swish, gold curtains fill the proscenium, heralding "The Morecambe & Wise Show" on BBC TV. ERIC *and* ERNIE *walk forward and play to both the cameras and studio audience.*

ERIC/ERNIE
BRING ME SUNSHINE, IN YOUR SMILE
BRING ME LAUGHTER, ALL THE WHILE
IN THIS WORLD WHERE WE LIVE
THERE SHOULD BE MORE HAPPINESS
SO MUCH JOY YOU CAN GIVE
TO EACH BRAND NEW, BRIGHT TOMORROW

MAKE ME HAPPY
THROUGH THE YEARS
NEVER BRING ME ANY TEARS
IN THIS WORLD WHERE WE LIVE
THERE SHOULD BE MORE HAPPINESS
BRING ME FUN, BRING ME SUNSHINE
BRING ME LOVE, SWEET LOVE
BRING ME FUN, BRING ME SUNSHINE
BRING ME LOVE.

ERNIE Good evening.

ERIC Is it?

ERNIE Eric, say "good evening" to the nice ladies and gentlemen.

ERIC If I could see any, I would.

ERNIE What about your loyal fans?

ERIC *(to audience)* Why, have they let him out?

ERNIE Aren't you thrilled to be back?

ERIC In my condition, I'm thrilled to be anything!

ERNIE As I was saying; a very warm welcome to the *(sic)* Workham and Mise...

ERIC *pounces upon* ERNIE*'s slight fluff.*

ERIC "Workham and Mise"? Who are they, your accountants?

ERNIE I meant to say "Morecambe and Wise".

ERIC But you didn't though, did you?

ERNIE Alas not.

ERIC How are the new teeth?

ERNIE Not quite broken in.

ERIC Why don't you see if you can borrow Nobby Stiles's? Nobby's gnashers would suit you to a tee, Ern. Tea urn! Wahey! How does he do it!? *(To audience)* How do we do it? If we have a secret at all, it's just that we've stuck together, eh, pally? Butter and crumpets, Pearl and Dean, Eric and Ernie. Dafter than doughnuts, as British as bank holidays. Cheeky asides, never saucier than a seaside postcard; a song and a dance, and we only mock the strong, NEVER the weak. A genius director, Johnny Ammonds, *and* a brilliant writer, Eddie Braben, ex-Liverpool market trader. Eddie's plums may be fingered and his banana bruised, but his gags are as ripe as raspberries. Even though he's never written a sketch in his life, Eddie shakes his sieve and comes up with gold...

EDDIE BRABEN *chats to* **ERIC** *and* **ERNIE** *in his soft Liverpudlian accent.*

EDDIE BRABEN Ernie, why don't we give you a new persona? Vain, snooty, thrifty... A comic who reckons he's funny, but isn't. A deluded playwright blessed with literary talent like what no-one has got. You can bounce off that, Eric... The odd wink to camera, "in on the gag" with the folks at home, mischievous as you like...

ERIC I like. I like. I like.

EDDIE BRABEN And every week, you star in your own mini-sitcom; the pair of you sharing a flat... a *bedroom* in a flat... A *bed* in a bedroom in a flat!

ERIC Sharing a bed?!

EDDIE BRABEN If it was good enough for Laurel and Hardy, it's good enough for you two!

ERIC *passes* ERNIE *back through the gold drapes, taking a newspaper in return and quoting some stellar reviews.*

ERIC "The combination is brilliant, wholly original and irresistible"... "They seem more like brothers than two comics"... "The first double act who look like they've got a proper relationship"...

Produces a small paper bag from his pocket.

As a famous human cannonball once told me, "you won't land anywhere, sunshine, 'till you've flown through the air first".

He throws up an imaginary ball and, with a yodelled "whoo-oo-oop!", flicks a finger against the bag, pretending to have caught it.

We've done a lot of flying, me and Ern, but now we've hit the target, boots on the bullseye. We win our second BAFTA and *I* get voted...

Reaches back between drapes, collecting an ornate pipe.

"Pipe Smoker Of The Year". My doctors say I must avoid any further excitement so I start watching Luton Town F.C. Well, if I drop down dead on the terraces at least it'd give 'em something to lift at the end of the season. They even make me an honorary director! Not bad for the newest member of the "Coronary Club", eh? Reg Varney, Sid James, Peter Sellers may have all jumped the queue but would they ever taste those fizzy joys of finishing sixth in the Second Division?

He shouts between the drapes.

All you stars of stage and screen form an orderly queue for a shaft of shared limelight, happy to be humiliated... Glenda Jackson has agreed to expose her foibles – she'd better watch out, there's a cold frost on the way... Shirley Bassey wants to sing "Smoke Gets In Your Eyes" – as long as she does it in size-ten hobnails... And André Previn will play Grieg's Piano Concerto. The heck he will... *I* will.

Perches grandly on the seats as if sitting on a piano stool.

Ladies and gentlemen, "The Liberace of Lancashire" will perform a unique arrangement – in Imperial weights and measures, with the second movement in old money. I thank you...

MUSIC: Truly awful piano playing – Grieg crucified.

ERIC *mimes along.*

All the right notes...

ERIC/AUDIENCE ...but not necessarily in the right order!

ERIC Top that Mr Preview! A-2-3-4...

MUSIC: truly beautiful piano playing – Grieg resurrected.

Rubbish. *(To audience)* By guesting on our show, the nation sees you as a good egg. And there are *baskets* of good eggs – Laurence Olivier, Vanessa Redgrave, Tom Jones, Cliff Richard, Sacha Distel, Sasha Disgrace... "Sasha Disgrace"? Sorry – Des O'Connor. No, no, I shouldn't be cruel about Des, even though his record company have been so cruel to so many. When I had my heart attack Des stopped his show in Paignton and asked the entire audience to say a prayer for me. I told him later, "those six or seven people made all the difference". 1971, BAFTA number four; '72, number five; '73... No more please, the mantelpiece won't take it! Joan and I award ourselves. We adopt a son. Stephen is four years old and loves watching me fishing. More time for... Time. We're all ticking along nicely...

Sound effects: A clock ticks.

Just past New Year, '76, my father is sitting in his favourite armchair, finishing supper and watching television. He stands up, tells my mum it's time for bed, and...

The clock suddenly stops.

...the doctors say that he was dead before he hit the carpet. Mum clings on. She tries living on her own, but it's no good. Without George Bartholomew, life is one grim, cold, endless winter, and all the time she tells me...

SADIE You know he's up there waiting for me, don't you?

ERIC *(to audience)* Her heart is shattered and all around it, her body starts to fall apart. Too frail to live alone, she comes to stay with us. One night, while I'm appearing in Manchester, Joan says Mum won't rest 'till I'm safe home. I streak down the M.1. quicker than Concorde, reaching Harpenden in the small hours, tip-toe upstairs and put my head around her bedroom door. Through the soft light, I can just make out her eyes opening. She smiles…having waited for me all that time to arrive and lets herself fall asleep for the last time…

MUSIC: "BY THE LIGHT OF THE SILVERY MOON" – gently reprises.

ERIC *gazes up to the heavens.*

…there she goes! Sadie Bartholomew – re-arranging the planets and getting Gemini to start a double-act. And there's old George, clocking in for his night shift… "Double-time for fillin' in potholes on t' Milky Way, son".

ERIC *waves farewell.*

I tell my own kids, "when you die, there's one up there for each of us. Stars…" That's what they're calling Ernie and I now. OBEs, honorary degrees, keys to the City Of London… Forty-odd years me and Ern have been together. Two sparks off the same flint, a smouldering dream that one day we'd light up the galaxy.

Sound effects: sleighbells.

ERIC *disappears behind the theatre seats, removing his tux and pulling on a cuddly pullover.*

Sound effects: **BBC TV ANNOUNCER** *(pre-recorded).*

BBC ANNOUNCER *(voiceover)* It's Christmas Day, 1977, and a stellar line-up here on BBC One: at seven fifteen, *The Generation Game* – festive family fun hosted by Brucey. Eight twenty, Mike Yarwood, "The King of Impersonations"…

ERIC Including one of me!

ANNOUNCER And, at five to nine, the show we've all been waiting for as Eric and Ernie present their biggest and best Christmas extravaganza. Star guests and great comic entertainment with the true kings of British comedy.

ERIC The cast of *Dad's Army* are standing by – I'm surprised they can manage it! Penelope Keith is willing – I thought she was spoken for! And Elton John's able. So I've heard! *(Offstage)* Stick the news on, would you love?

Sound effects: news sting/ NEWSREADER *(pre-recorded).*

NEWSREADER Today in the headlines, Charlie Chaplin dies at the age of 88, Israel and Egypt hold peace talks and twenty-eight million, eight hundred and seventy-five thousand people tune in to *The Morecambe And Wise Christmas Show* – over half the country...

ERIC *(to audience)* If only we'd bought shares in Watney's Party Seven or ready salted crisps! One hour and ten minutes of celestial supremacy. But it also marks the very last show we make for the BBC. The bigger a star, the hotter it gets and the hotter it gets, the quicker it dies... Thames TV make us an offer we can't refuse and even promise us a feature film. Our "Rank efforts" in the '60s hadn't fared so well, one critic imploring: "Norman Wisdom please come back!" Now, we can bounce back, eh Ern?

ERNIE *has been pre-set back on the prop trunk down stage right.*

ERNIE Rubber balls.

ERIC *grabs* ERNIE*'s lapels playfully.*

ERIC I'll smash yer face in...

*MUSIC: a slow, gentle **"TAKE ME OUT TO THE BALL GAME".***

Home... Harpenden. A winter morning. Wogan on the radio, my two lads are on their toast and a roast chicken squats on a shelf in the fridge, waiting to be picked and nibbled. It's nice to be home...

Suddenly, he grimaces and clutches his chest. He falls.

When my boys hear the crash and see me prostrate hanging on to a chicken leg, they think I'm mucking about. But for once I'm deadly serious. A second heart attack, and as the old song goes: "It's one, two, three strikes you're out at the old ball game"...

Crawls to the seats, gathering himself.

I joke about the triple bypass, that my scar looks like the "mark of Zorro" and my biggest threat came from the hospital cocoa. But in truth, it's my confidence that's taken the brunt. If I meet someone, I shield the left hand side of my body, get twitchy I'll get bumped and have another attack...be still my Achilles heart. Comedy is a confidence trick, and when I can finally face work again, the difference is plain to see...

Takes off his cardigan, replaces it with tux and tie.

What I'm really trying to say is that the word 'yes' is a reaction... "Yes, we'd love to", "yes please", "yes thanks", "oh yes!" "Yes, yes, yes!"

Sound effects: **BILLY MARSH** *(pre-recorded) speaks:*

BILLY Thames TV want one more, Eric.

ERIC A reflex...

BILLY One more.

ERIC Even for one who no longer needs money or the fame...

BILLY Just the Christmas show. Then you and Ernie can finish that new film of yours.

ERIC Even for one on a "Two Strike Warning".

BILLY You can say no, Eric.

ERIC *(laughs)* You reckon, Billy? Eh?

MUSIC: *silent movie-type piano.*

(To audience) The '83 Christmas show. Ern and I as The Keystone Cops, back on the slapstick beat...

From the trunk, he picks up a cop's helmet and truncheon.

We know the drill. The classic chase: run hell-for-leather at that brick wall then slam on the brake at the last minute so they can get the scissors in for the "wallop". Meat and drink to Ern, me and Fatty Arbuckle...

He moves in slow motion.

Only a short distance, not gonna kill you. Run, fella, run... Almost there... Now stop, fella, STOP... Is my timing out? Maybe it's the floor or I'm dazzled by the lights, but I can't stop... I can't stop... I CAN'T...

Sound effects: a crash.

ERIC *crumples in a heap down stage centre.*

(To audience) I hit the scenery so hard it knocks my heart out of rhythm. Hospital for two days. If there'd been writing on that wall it would have said, "one more Christmas show and that's your lot, Morecambe".

Stands gingerly, dusting himself down. Taking in his surroundings, he pops the helmet and truncheon into the trunk.

We muddle through the film Thames had promised us. The so-called "thriller", *Night Train To Murder* is so bad, I plead for it never to be released. *(To* **ERNIE***)* So much for our Hollywood dream, pally. It's funny, our double act was born on trains, and looks like it might have died on one. We ran the red signal a good ways back. Some ride, though, eh? Full steam ahead for forty-three years, give or take the odd points failure. You always joked that I was the "show" and you were the "business". Well, the show has finally beaten me. I don't want to drop down dead on stage like Tommy Cooper. I long for an espresso in Rome or smell the summer rain in Venice, drive through the burning fall from Maine to Florida, get closer to my wife and kids and properly get to know my grandchildren. I want to watch an osprey pull a salmon from a shining loch, then land one bigger myself... And I want to write more: novels and kids' stories, fishing books... I might even see the Hatters win the cup final! Infinite possibilities, in"this world where we live"...

Gazes at the little stage, the prop trunk and theatre seats with a poignant smile.

(To audience) "The Show". At three years old, a penny a song to the gang on a building site, at six, a dab of sherbert for a joke. Where does it come from? When does it stop? If I don't stop it, *it's* going to stop *me*. It won't be easy. How do you kill second nature; that instinct to get a laugh and go after another like a ratter's terrier? Never mind "on stage" – on the riverbank, at a petrol pump, even stood in the gents. "Yes, young man, I am Eric Morecambe. You'd like to shake my *what?*" An autograph would fade, a picture curl up and get torn…but giving someone a laugh was a memento which I hoped might last them a lifetime. If I made *you* laugh, all well and good. If I made you care, even better. Soon, they'll be locking up, turning out these lights and sweeping the stage, ready for the next show in the big, dark room where all the trouble started. I don't want any more trouble…

MUSIC: "THE CURTAIN FALLS".

As **ERIC** *sings, he dons the mac and flat cap we first saw him wearing.*

OFF COMES THE MAKE-UP
OFF COMES THE CLOWN'S DISGUISE
THE MUSIC'S ENDING
THE LAUGHTER SLOWLY DIES
BUT I HOPE YOU'RE SMILING
AS YOU'RE FILING OUT THE DOOR
AS THEY SAY IN THIS BIZ
"THAT'S ALL THERE IS"
THERE ISN'T ANY MORE…

Takes a Luton Town F.C. scarf from his coat pocket and wraps it proudly around his neck.

WE SHARED A MOMENT
AND AS THAT MOMENT ENDS
I'VE GOT A FUNNY FEELING
WE'RE PARTING NOW AS FRIENDS

YOUR TEARS AND LAUGHTER
WILL LINGER AFTER
THEY'VE TORN DOWN THESE DUSTY WALLS
IF I HAD THIS TO DO AGAIN

Picks up **ERNIE** *one last time.*

IF THE EVENING WERE NEW AGAIN
I WOULD SPEND IT WITH YOU AGAIN...

Tenderly kisses **ERNIE**, *placing him back into the trunk, closing the lid.*

BUT NOW THE CURTAIN FALLS...
YOUR CHEERS AND LAUGHTER
WILL LINGER AFTER
THEY'VE TORN DOWN THESE DUSTY WALLS...

Unable to resist one last wisecrack, he inches forward into the spotlight down stage centre.

There's a famous one-armed commissionaire at the BBC Television Centre. Every day he holds the door open for us. One day, he says to me, "Mr Morecambe, can I have two tickets for me and the wife for the show Saturday night?". I say, "No". He says, "why not?". I say, "because you can't clap"...

Picks up his suitcase, set to continue his onward journey.

(Sings)

PEOPLE SAY I WAS MADE FOR THIS,
NOTHING MORE WOULD I TRADE FOR THIS
AND TO THINK I GET PAID FOR THIS...

Sound effects: **SADIE**'*s voice (pre-recorded).*

SADIE Jifflearse!

ERIC Mum?

SADIE Jifflearse! Get off! Leave 'em wanting more...

Sound effects: an ambulance siren.

ERIC *stares towards a far-off horizon.*

ERIC He's not going to sell much ice-cream going at that
speed...

Blackout.

An instrumental **MUSIC: "BRING ME SUNSHINE"** *rings
out.* ERIC *re-enters carrying* ERNIE. *After taking their curtain
calls they "Groucho dance" off into immortality.*

FURNITURE & PROPERTY LIST

The action takes place on a stage dressed to evoke the interior of a vintage music hall, a theatrical props trunk D.S.R. and (twin) plush theatre seats D.S.L. alongside a side table, with a coat stand and tailor's mannequin behind. A small raised platform with false proscenium, velvet curtains and footlights forms a separate playing area U.S.C. As each designer must be allowed to bring their own ingenuity to the staging, the following is intended to be instructive rather than prescriptive:

Theatrical props trunk (p1)
Twin plush theatre seats (p1)
Side table (p1)
Coat stand (p1)
Tailor's mannequin – female torso (p1)
Stepladder (p1)
Suitcase (p2)
Pipe (p1/39/40)
Mannequin leg – pink bow attached (p2)
Bottle of Johnnie Walker whisky/glass (p2)
Human skull (p2)
Des O'Connor album (p3)
Ventriloquist's doll – a perfect likeness of ERNIE WISE (p3)
Ukulele (p7)
Walking cane (p7)
Telegram (p7)
Chromatic harmonica (p7)
Blanket (p9)
Sadie's letter (p17)
Briefcase (p19)
Vintage radio (p21)
Newspaper/s (p25/27/43)
Overlong false leg – with shoe/sock-suspender (p29)
Red telephone receiver (p33)
Prescription (p40)
Pill jar containing four tablets (p40)
Small fridge (p40)
Gold curtains bearing "M&W" logo (p41)
Small paper bag (p43)
Ornate pipe (p43)
Cop's helmet and truncheon (p47)

COSTUME:
Specific costume requirements/suggestions are noted within the text.

SOUND EFFECTS

(Pre-recorded off-stage voices):
Radio pips/BBC NEWSREADER (p1/46)
LIVERPUDLIAN M.C. (p6)
SCOTTISH M.C. (p11)
GRUBBY CLUB COMPERE (p18)
ERIC's voice on radio (p21)
ED SULLIVAN (p35)
BBC ANNOUNCER (p24/45)
BILLY MARSH (p47)
ERNIE (p36/37)
SADIE (p50)

(Off-stage sounds):

The following are open to interpretation, editing or embellishment if required:

Applause/cheers/laughter/stomping/groans (p4 and throughout)
Descending bomb/bomb explodes (p8)
Door knock (p9)
Thunder and lightning (p11)
Lonesome wind (p12)
Solemn church bell (p12)
Phone ring (p14/23 29 33)
Steam train (p15/16)
Hammers and picks (p15)
Music hall atmosphere (p19)
Breaking china (p23)
Baby cries (p24/29)
Cymbal crash/ applause (p24/31)
Thud/woman's scream (p29)
Idling taxi (p30)
Drum fill (p34)
Timpani roll (p35)
Seagulls, waves, funfair sounds (p35)

Atomic explosion (p36)
Birdsong (p39)
Ticking clock (p44)
Sleighbells (p45)
Crash (p48)
Ambulance siren (p50)

LIGHTING

The lighting state creates a rarified, ethereal atmosphere – time
transfixed (p1)
Houselights go down (p1)
Blackout (p28/51)
Specific follow-spot/specials cues, etc. are highlighted within the
text.

PERFORMED SONGS

Having received permission from the relevant publishing
companies, the author gratefully includes the lyrics to the
following compositions:

"Positive Thinking"– Tony Hatch/Jackie Trent.
© Copyright 1974 (p28)

"Bring Me Sunshine" – words by Sylvia Dee/music by Arthur Kent.
© Copyright 1966 Music Sales Corporation/Campbell Connelly &
Co. (p41)All Rights Reserved. International Copyright Secured.
Used by permission of Chester Music Limited trading as
Campbell Connelly & Co.

"The Curtain Falls"– Sol Weinstein.
© Copyright Warner Chappell Ltd. ©1962 WB Music Corp
(ASCAP)All rights reserved by Warner /Chappell North America
Ltd (p49/ 50)

Previous productions of MORECAMBE have relied upon the
services of a musical director/associate to realise each song's
arrangement - whether as an orchestrated backing track or
performed live with minimal instrumentation.

INCIDENTAL MUSIC

The following short instrumental cues are included as suggestions only:

"I'm Knee Deep In Daisies" (p8)
"Spanish Gypsy Dance" (P8)
"By The Light Of The Silvery Moon" (p10/45)
"Carmina Burana" (p11)
"Scotland The Brave" (p11)
"Reveille" (p15)
"Bring Me Sunshine" (p15/16/41)
"The Woody Woodpecker Song" (p20)
"The Wedding March" (p23)
"Following You Around" (p29)
'Two of A Kind" (P34)
"The Stripper" (p40)
"Also Spracht Zarathustra" (p40)
Grieg's Piano Concerto in A minor (p44)
"Take Me Out To The Ball game" (p46)

(Stings – either sourced or specifically composed):

Vaudeville-type sting (p10)
Seedy nightclub piano (p17)
Romantic waltz (p22)
Celeste underscore (p25)
James Bond-type sting (p32)
Brassy walk-on sting (p32)
Fanfare (p36)
Silent movie-type piano (p47)

Lightning Source UK Ltd.
Milton Keynes UK
UKHW020333191218
334251UK00005B/168/P